Sometimes at school I'm afraid of the big kids. I feel better when I talk to my mom or dad or teacher about it.

I used to be scared that there were things in my closet or under my bed. Now I check both places before I turn off the lights.

Thinking about ghosts and skeletons really frightens me. But my mom always says, "Nothing can hurt you. I'm right here."

Bobbi Katz

# An Invitation

Let's be spooky. Let's have fun!
We'll scare ourselves before we're done
with ghosts and goblins — winds that howl —
things that fly and things that prowl.
We'll talk about such creepy stuff
until we both get scared enough
to hear things that we cannot see
and see things that just cannot be.
Let's be spooky — you and me.

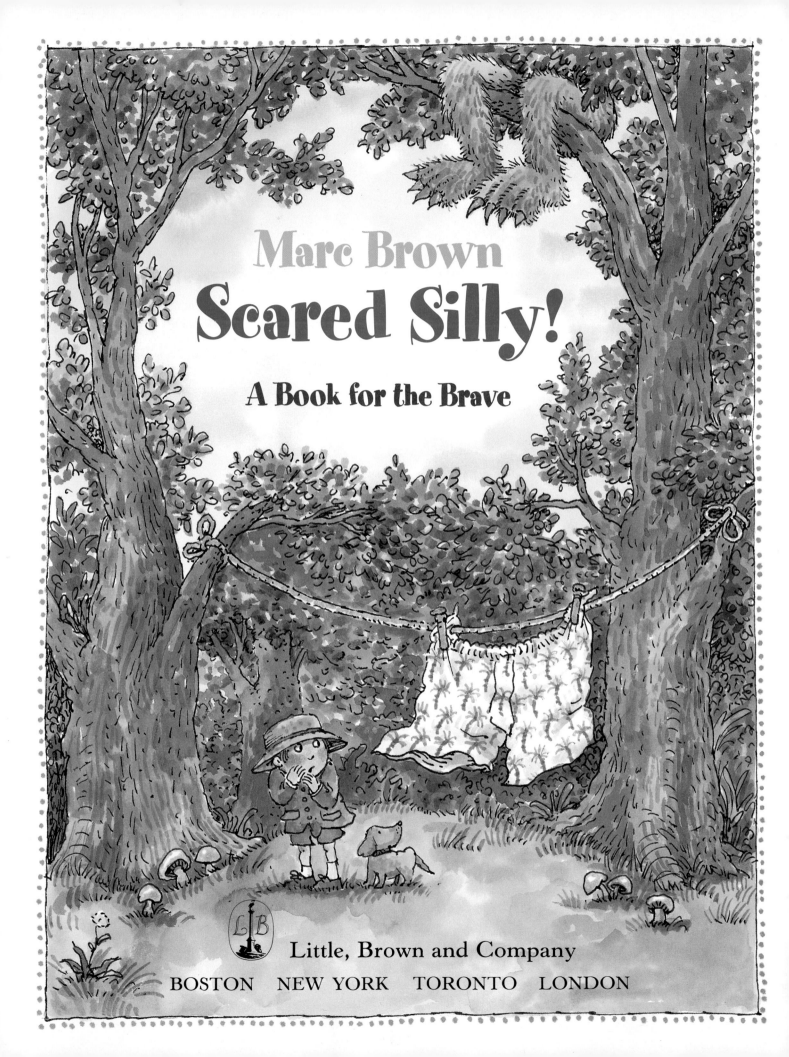

# Marc Brown
# Scared Silly!

## A Book for the Brave

Little, Brown and Company

BOSTON   NEW YORK   TORONTO   LONDON

For Judith Stolp, Derby Academy kindergarten teacher,
in whose class *Scared Silly!* happened

First Edition

Copyright acknowledgments appear on page 61.

Library of Congress Cataloging-in-Publication Data

Scared silly! : a book for the brave
  / [compiled and illustrated by] Marc Brown ; with a foreword by Robert Coles.
  — 1st ed.
      p.      cm.
   Summary: An illustrated collection of spooky stories, poems, and
riddles including a humorous array of ghosts, monsters, ghouls, and
witches.
   ISBN 0-316-11360-3
   1. Children's literature.    [1. Literature — Collections.]
I. Brown, Marc Tolon, ill.
PZ5.S317   1994
810.8'09282 — dc20                                            93-13501
              10   9   8   7   6   5   4   3
                              SC
Published simultaneously in Canada
by Little, Brown & Company (Canada) Limited
Printed in Hong Kong

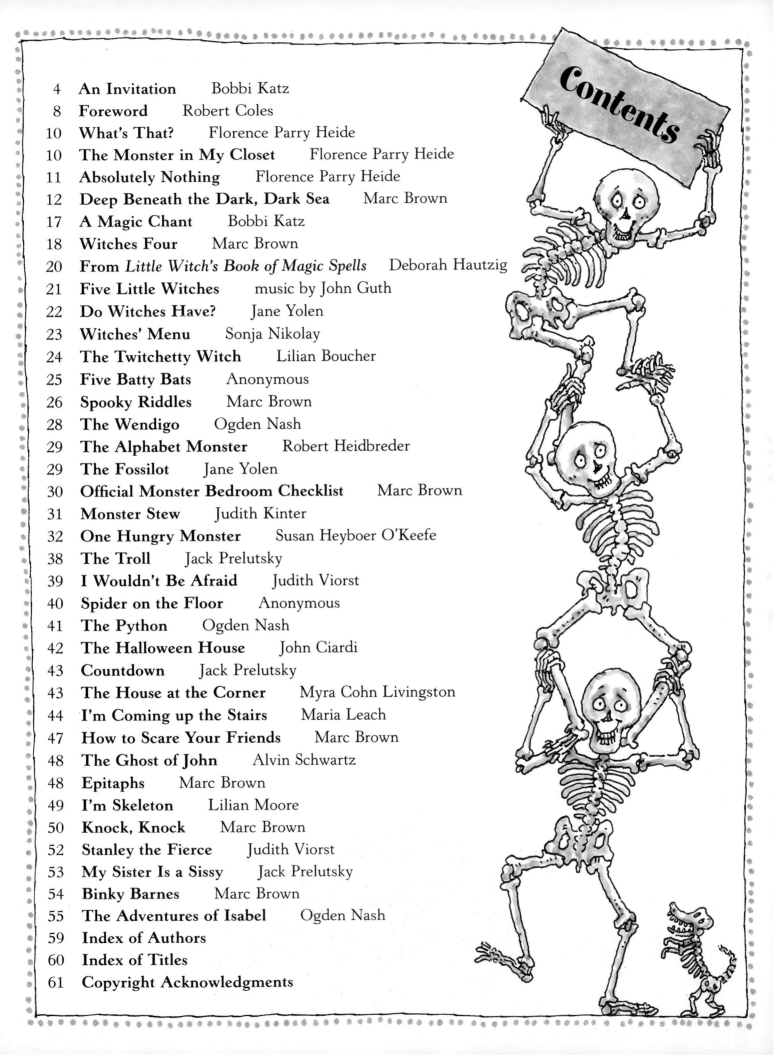

# Contents

# Foreword

For all of us — grown-up and child — fear and worry live intimately with the excitement and pleasure offered by daily experience. Again and again the world offers its new challenges, its inducements and promises and thrills. Yet we tremble and feel afraid — and why not! Who knows what step will turn into a misstep? For children, such a line of reasoning is not directly posed but is known in the bones, the gut — that place in all of us where factuality gives way to intuition: I *sense* something.

I recall a child of eight with whom I was working as a child psychiatrist-in-training. The boy kept telling me how frightened he was of all sorts of events, incidents, and phenomena, to the point that I remarked, "Gerry, you seem very distrustful of just about everything!" He hesitated not a second to shoot back, "Well, it's because I'd like to do so *much!*" It took me a while to understand what he had tried to say — that his so-called phobias were prompted by the ever growing number of invitations the world was sending his way: Here, try this; consider that; and look, there's something else.

So it goes as bodies and minds grow in competence. With this growth, the parameters of possibility expand and so, too, the chances that trouble may occur. *Some* fear, then, is not a cause for parental alarm, but rather is a sign in children of thoughtfulness, of a boy's, a girl's, willingness to take the measure of things.

This is what *Scared Silly!* will help parents and children alike to do: acknowledge the natural fears we all have as we struggle with the darkness both within us (our various lusts, drives, urges) and without (the frustrations, irritations, impasses, puzzles, and dangers that the world presents from time to time). The title Marc Brown has given to this wonderfully entertaining, suggestive, and gently provocative collection of stories and poems is right on target. Just around the corner from apprehension and anxiety are to be found the exuberance, the giddiness, the mastery, that go with a series of successful experiences, that go with forays into the unknown and untried. Children gradually, eventually learn (and will be helped to learn as they go through this book) that it is silly to be endlessly scared. But before such knowledge is obtained, both children and their parents have to acknowledge what being "scared" is about: a testing of the waters before the plunge — and then the silliness, meaning, "See what I know now, what I can do now, *silly!*" We all learn to address ourselves this way. We all (with caution and desire, both) learn to take on this world, to get some sense of confidence about it, control over it — and this book will be a fine companion for many young people who are just starting to do so.

Robert Coles

## What's That?

Florence Parry Heide

What's that?
Who's there?
There's a great huge horrible *horrible*
creeping up the stair!
A huge big terrible *terrible*
with creepy crawly hair!
There's a ghastly grisly *ghastly*
with seven slimy eyes!
And flabby grabby tentacles
of a gigantic size!
He's crept into my room now,
he's leaning over me.
I wonder if he's thinking
how delicious I will be.

Florence Parry Heide

## The Monster in My Closet

The monster in my closet
hides there just for fun.
He shrieks and moans and rattles bones
just like a skeleton.
He always tries to scare me
(he does it as a joke).
But tonight I shouted BOO! at him
and he went up in smoke!

Florence Parry Heide

# Absolutely Nothing

Dinosaurs . . .
They're very, very dead, you know.
They died a zillion years ago. . . .
But whether they're alive or dead,
there's one that hides beneath my bed.
His teeth are huge. He has big scales.
His toenails are as sharp as nails.
I hear him breathe. I hear him snore.
I hear him gnash his teeth and roar.

My mother says, "Look here, my dear,
there's *absolutely nothing* here!"

He's getting very hungry now. . . .
He'll have to get a meal somehow.

My father says, "There's nothing there.
There's *absolutely nothing* there!"

But in the morning they will see
*absolutely nothing*
            left of me!

Marc Brown
# Deep Beneath the Dark, Dark Sea

Under the dark, dark sky was a deep, deep ocean.
And on that deep, deep ocean were cold, cold waves.

And beneath those cold, cold waves lay an old, old shipwreck.
And inside the old, old shipwreck swam a deadly, deadly octopus.

And around the deadly, deadly octopus grew thick, thick weeds.
And within the thick, thick weeds sat a white, white skeleton.

And beside the white, white skeleton was a black, black trunk.
And from inside the black, black trunk
Shot a hungry, hungry shark!

I was really scared of him
And discovered how fast I could swim!

Bobbi Katz
# A Magic Chant

Mumbo jumbo griggle grumbo!
Fista fasta lasta pasta!
Joga voga foga Voo!
Ickle pickle parsley stew!

Say these words by day or night.
Get them absolutely right.
Learn them and you'll be prepared
For anything that makes you scared.

Mumbo jumbo griggle grumbo!
Fista fasta lasta pasta!
Joga voga foga Voo!
Ickle pickle parsley stew!

Marc Brown

# Witches Four

One witch,
two witches,
three witches,
four.
Not one less, not one more.
Everyone calls them WITCHES FOUR.

They each wear spectacles on their nose.
They dance together on forty toes.

They brush their teeth with spider paste.
They eat bat-wing sandwiches.
They like the taste!

Witch boots on,
tied-up laces.
Frog-eye soap
to wash their faces.

Witches . . .
one,
two,
three,
four . . .
dressed for spooking
and out the door.

They each take out a magic broom.
They click their heels,
and off they zoom!

Deborah Hautzig

# From Little Witch's
# Book of Magic Spells

Twiggly, wiggly
Creepy tree,
Make a tree house
Just for me.

Yappy, snappy
Growling dog,
You will be
A friendly frog!

Ooky, spooky
Cloudy night,
Stars come out
And shine your light.

# Five Little Witches

Music by John Guth

Five lit - tle wit - ches on a Hal - lo - ween night made a ver - y, ver - y

spook - y sight. The

first witch danced on her tip - py tip - toes. The

sec - ond witch tum - bled and bumped her nose. The

third witch flew high up in the air. The

fourth witch combed her fuz - zy hair. The

fifth witch sang a Hal - lo - ween song.

Five wit - ches played the whole night long!

Jane Yolen

# Do Witches Have?

Do witches have babies?
    No, witches have toads.
    They find them in wellsprings
    Or on country roads.

Do witches have babies?
    No, witches have cats
    Who sleep amongst broomstraws
    Or curl up in hats.

Do witches have babies?
    No, witches have snakes
    That twine around broomsticks
    Or vampire stakes.

Do witches have babies?
    Of course witches do.
    If we don't have babies —
    Then how come there's you?

Sonja Nikolay

# Witches' Menu

Live lizard, dead lizard
Marinated, fried.
Poached lizard, pickled lizard
Salty lizard hide.

Hot lizard, cold lizard
Lizard over ice.
Baked lizard, boiled lizard
Lizard served with spice.

Sweet lizard, sour lizard
Smoked lizard heart.
Leg of lizard, loin of lizard
Lizard a la carte.

Lilian Boucher

# The Twitchetty Witch

A Twitchetty Witch
Went hurtling by,
Twitchetty, Witchetty,
Yooo-hooo-hooo!
Up in the dark
Where the black bats fly,
With her pointed nose
And her glittering eye,
A Twitchetty Witch
Went hurtling by,
Twitchetty, Witchetty —
S-w-w-i-i-i-s-shh!

Anonymous
# Five Batty Bats

Five batty bats
Were hanging 'neath the moon.

"Quiet!" said the first.
"The witch is coming soon."

"She's green," said the second,
"With a purple pointy nose."

"Black boots," said the third,
"Cover up her ugly toes."

"Her broom," said the fourth,
"Can scratch you — that I know!"

"I'm scared," said the fifth.
"I think we'd better go."

Five batty bats
Escaped into the night.

"Dear me," said the witch.
"That's a scary sight!"

Marc Brown
# Spooky Riddles

How do you unlock a haunted house?

With a skeleton key.

What dessert do ghosts like best?

Booberry pie with I scream.

What do you get if you cross a cucumber with a werewolf?

A pickle that gets hairy when there's a full moon.

When is it unlucky to be followed by a black cat?

When you're a mouse.

Why couldn't the witches play baseball?

They couldn't find the bats.

What subject do little witches like best?

Spelling.

Where do cowboy goblins live?

In ghost towns.

Why do witches wear black capes?

Because they get too hot when they werewolf.

## Ogden Nash
# The Wendigo

The Wendigo,
The Wendigo!
Its eyes are ice and indigo!
Its blood is rank and yellowish!
Its voice is hoarse and bellowish!
Its tentacles are slithery,
And scummy,
Slimy,
Leathery!
Its lips are hungry blubbery,
And smacky,
Sucky,
Rubbery!
The Wendigo,
The Wendigo!
I saw it just a friend ago!
Last night it lurked in Canada;
Tonight, on your veranada!
As you are lolling hammockwise,
It contemplates you stomachwise.
You loll,
It contemplates,
It lollops.
The rest is merely gulps
  and gollops.

Robert Heidbreder
# The Alphabet Monster

I'm the Alphabet Monster
And nothing tastes better
To the Alphabet Monster
Than eating a letter.
A *J* and an *a*
And a *c* and a *k*
And the million more letters
I munch every day.

I'm hungry now.
What shall I do?
I think I'll eat
a *y*
an *o*
and a *u* —

That means . . . YOU!

Jane Yolen
# The Fossilot

You cannot find a Fossilot
Except in ancient stones,
Where imprints of its teeth and claws
Lie jumbled with its bones.

Some scientists cleaned up the bones,
Arranged, then tried to date them.
But when they had the jaw complete —
It turned around and ate them.

## Official Monster Bedroom Checklist

1. Check under the bed (use a flashlight).
2. Check under the covers.
3. Check behind the curtains.
4. Look in the closets.
5. Check all toy areas.
6. Get into bed.
7. Relax.
8. Sweet dreams.

Judith Kinter
# Monster Stew

If you are getting tired
Of plain old witches' brew,
Next time you have a party
Try gourmet monster stew.

Put on an old black apron
Borrowed from a witch;
Then scoop in murky water
From a brackish ditch.

Pond slime is the next thing,
A bucketful or two;
But if you don't have pond slime,
Some moldy soup will do.

Now measure in an owl-hoot,
Two grumbles and a groan.
To make it really tasty,
Add an eerie moan.

Now if your guests are monsters,
You cackle while they eat.
They'll say your stew is gruesome,
A most delightful treat!

Susan Heyboer O'Keefe

# One Hungry Monster

One hungry monster
underneath my bed,
moaning and groaning
and begging to be fed.

Two hungry monsters
at my closet door,
chewing up my sneakers,
asking me for more.

Three hungry monsters
in the upstairs hall,
lick the flower painting
hanging on the wall.

Four hungry monsters
'round my daddy's head,
sniffing out the crackers
he'd eaten in his bed.

Five hungry monsters
sliding down the rail,
munching and crunching
on one another's tail.

Six hungry monsters
underneath the rug,
tracking down some footprints
to catch a tasty bug.

Seven hungry monsters
'round our TV screen,
drooling at commercials
for sauerkraut and beans.

Eight hungry monsters
on the chandeliers
swear they haven't eaten
for maybe twenty years.

Nine hungry monsters
wearing roller skates,
hunting through the kitchen
for knives and forks and plates.

Ten hungry monsters
about to fuss and kick,
won't get out, they tell me,
unless I feed them quick!

So I bring out 1 jug of apple juice,
2 loaves of bread,
3 bowls of spaghetti
that they dump upon my head,
4 purple eggplants,
5 pickled pears,
6 orange pumpkins
they climb up and down like stairs,
7 roasted turkeys,
8 pizza pies,
9 watermelons
that they wish were twice the size,
10 jars of peanut butter,
but not a speck of jam
('cause I want every monster mouth
shut tighter than a clam).

They gargle with some apple juice,
then shower with the rest.

They pinch the bread to bread crumbs
and won't clean up their mess.

They braid the spaghetti into wigs
and eat the eggplants whole,
and learn that pickled pears
won't bounce —
and neither will they roll.

They wear the pumpkin tops as hats
and dream of pumpkin pie.
They argue over wishbones
and pick the turkeys dry.

They toss the pizzas back and forth
like Frisbees through the air,
then spit out sticky melon seeds
to land right in my hair.

They paint the peanut butter
like lipstick on their mouths,
then stamp their feet and loudly say,
"What ELSE is in this house?"

"Get out, get out!"
I loudly shout.
"You've made a mess
and then, no less,
you ate my food,
and were quite rude.
You put me in
a nasty mood.
You are so bad
it makes me mad!

"It makes me want
to squirm and twist,
to make a face,
and shake my fist,
to stamp the floor
and kick the door,
and then do it
all once more!
And so without
a single doubt,
I tell you now —
get out, get out!"

Ten sorry monsters
creeping one by one,
climb up the chimney,
and now my job is done.

Then from behind the toaster,
my secret hiding spot,
I take an apple muffin
the monsters never got!

•37•

Jack Prelutsky

# The Troll

Be wary of the loathsome troll
that slyly lies in wait
to drag you to his dingy hole
and put you on his plate.

His blood is black and boiling hot,
he gurgles ghastly groans.
He'll cook you in his dinner pot,
your skin, your flesh, your bones.

He'll catch your arms and clutch your legs
and grind you to a pulp,
then swallow you like scrambled eggs —
gobble! gobble! gulp!

So watch your steps when next you go
upon a pleasant stroll,
or you might end in the pit below
as supper for the troll.

Judith Viorst
# I Wouldn't Be Afraid

I wouldn't be afraid to fight a demon or a dragon,
    if you'd dare me.
I wouldn't be afraid of witches, warlocks, trolls, or giants.
Just worms scare me.

Anonymous

# Spider on the Floor

There's a spider on the floor,
There's a spider on the floor,
There's a spider on the floor.
Who could ask for anything more
Than a spider on the floor?

Now the spider's on my leg,
He's really, really big,
There's a spider on my leg.

Now the spider's on my stomach,
Oh, he's such a big old lummock,
There's a spider on my stomach.

Now the spider's on my neck,
Oh, I'm gonna be a wreck,
There's a spider on my neck!

Now the spider's on my face,
Oh, what a big disgrace,
There's a spider on my face!

Now the spider's on my head,
Oh, I wish that I were dead,
There's a spider on my head!

But he jumps off — *plop!*

Now there's a spider on the floor,
There's a spider on the floor,
There's a spider on the floor.
Who could ask for anything more
Than a spider on the floor?

Ogden Nash
# The Python

The python has, and I fib no fibs,
318 pairs of ribs.
In stating this I place reliance
On a seance with one who died for science.
This figure is sworn to and attested;
He counted them while being digested.

John Ciardi

# The Halloween House

I'm told there's a Green Thing in there.
And the sign on the gate says BEWARE!
   But of course it's not true.
   That's why I'm sending you
To sneak in and find out — *but take care!*

Jack Prelutsky
# Countdown

There are ten ghosts in the pantry,
There are nine upon the stairs,
There are eight ghosts in the attic,
There are seven on the chairs,
There are six within the kitchen,
There are five along the hall,
There are four upon the ceiling,
There are three upon the wall,
There are two ghosts on the carpet,
Doing things that ghosts will do,
There is one ghost
    right
        behind me
           Who is oh so quiet . . . . .

Myra Cohn Livingston
# The House at the Corner

The house at the corner
is cold gray stone,
where the trees and windows
crack and groan,
so I run past
    fast
      when I'm all alone.

Maria Leach

# I'm Coming up the Stairs

Once there was a little girl named Tilly who was afraid to go to bed. Nothing bad had ever happened to her, but somebody had told her some scary stories, and after that she was afraid.

One night she really did hear something. She lay in bed — listening — and she heard a very quiet voice say, "Tilly, I'm coming up the stairs."

The next night Tilly asked her mother if she could keep the light on for a while, but her mother said, "Nonsense, darling." Nothing happened that night, so Tilly did not ask again. But the next night while Tilly was lying in bed, afraid to go to sleep, she heard a little voice say, slowly, "Tilly, I'm on the first step."

Tilly was too scared to get up and look.

The next night she heard the little whispering voice say, "Tilly, I'm on the second step."

Tilly got more and more scared each night, but everybody told her, "Oh, that's nothing."

There were eight steps in the staircase; and every night Tilly heard the voice.

"Tilly, I'm on the third step" —

"Tilly, I'm on the fourth step" —

"Tilly, I'm on the fifth step" — until one night she heard the voice say, "Tilly, I'm in the hall."

Tilly was so frightened she couldn't eat her breakfast the next morning, and she couldn't eat her supper that night.

The next night Tilly was lying awake in bed, and it was not very long before she heard that horrid little whispering voice say, "Tilly, I'm at the door."

The next night it said, "Tilly, I'm *in the room!*"

Tilly was too scared even to scream for her mother.

The next night the voice said, "Tilly, I'm standing by the bed!" And the next night

Marc Brown
# How to Scare Your Friends

Sometimes it's fun to feel scared and be spooky. Here's a fun way to frighten your friends. Invite them to visit the Tomb of Gloom! One at a time, ask them to sit in a chair. Blindfold them, then dare them to touch the gruesome things from inside the Tomb. Only *you* know that things are not always what they seem!

| **eyeballs** | are really | two peeled grapes |
| **fingers** | are really | green beans |
| **teeth** | are really | dried kidney beans |
| **veins and arteries** | are really | cooked spaghetti in warm water |
| **vomit** | is really | cooked oatmeal |
| **ears** | are really | dried apricots |
| **guts** | are really | canned pork and beans |

If they make it through the Tomb of Gloom alive and are hungry for more, finish them off with a cup of human blood (tomato juice or milk with red food coloring) and a lizard skin cookie with frog eyeballs (green-colored sugar cookies with candy-coated chocolate bits). Or maybe they'd prefer a big spoonful of brains (Jell-O with fruit or marshmallows)?

Alvin Schwartz
# The Ghost of John

Have you seen the ghost of John?
Long white bones
and the flesh all g-o-n-e?
Oooooooooh!
Wouldn't it be chilly
with no skin o-n?

Marc Brown
# Epitaphs

Here lies what's left of little Jimmy Burdette He never read the directions to his chemistry set.

Here lies the body of Captain M. Moat He should have fixed that hole in his boat.

Here lies the body of DARCY DATORS Her big mistake was feeding those gators.

Lilian Moore

# I'm Skeleton

I'm the local Skeleton
who walks this
street.
This is my beat.
Beware!
I'm not very hairy
but I scare
*everyone* I meet.

People quiver
when they see me.
They flee me!
They shiver
if they must walk
alone.

Oops, there's a dog.
I must run.
His tail has a wag.
He wants to play tag.
And how he would like a
*bone!*

Here lies the
body of
Jolly Aunt Gert
she should have
said no to that tenth
dessert.

Here lies the body
of
Joshua Green
last seen
working the
sausage machine.

Here lies the body
of
Jenny Paine
she almost
learned how to
fly a plane.

Marc Brown
# Knock, Knock

Knock, knock.
Who's there?
Abra.
Abra who?
Abracadabra! I will now make you disappear!

Knock, knock.
Who's there?
Owl.
Owl who?
Owl huff and owl puff till I blow this door down!

Knock, knock.
Who's there?
Dawn.
Dawn who?
Dawn be frightened, it's just me!

Knock, knock.
Who's there?
Canoe.
Canoe who?
Canoe lend me a coat? I'm freezing!

Knock, knock.
Who's there?
Spider.
Spider who?
You tried to hide her, but I spider!

Knock, knock.
Who's there?
Dora.
Dora who?
Your dora bell was broken —
that's why I had to knock!

Judith Viorst

# Stanley the Fierce

Stanley the Fierce
Has a chipped front tooth
And clumps of spiky hair.
And his hands are curled into
      two fat fists
And his arms are bulgy and bare.
And his smile is a tight little
      mean little smile
And his eyes give a shivery glare.
And I hear that he goes for seventeen days
Without changing his underwear.

But I don't think I'll ask him.

Jack Prelutsky

# My Sister Is a Sissy

My sister is a sissy,
she's afraid of dogs and cats,
a toad can give her tantrums,
and she's terrified of rats,
she screams at things with stingers,
things that buzz, and things that crawl,
just the shadow of a spider
sends my sister up the wall.

A lizard makes her shiver,
and a turtle makes her squirm,
she positively cringes
at the prospect of a worm,
she's afraid of things with feathers,
she's afraid of things with fur,
she's scared of almost everything —
how come I'm scared of her?

Marc Brown

# Binky Barnes

When recess starts, I feel afraid.
There's this kid in second grade . . .

I hear he sat on Tom O'Connor.
If he sits on me, then I'm a goner!
He looks for kids to squish and crunch.
He said he'd find me after lunch!
They say he likes to pulverize.
Wish he'd pick on kids his size.
Of course, there are no kids that big.
I'll bet he snaps me like a twig.

Oh, no! He's coming over here!
I think I'm sick!
I think I'm sick!
He sees me now, he's almost here.
I'm going to die!
I'm going to die!

Uh-oh, he's standing next to me.
Should I even try to flee?
I'd better pray.
What did you say?
You want to play?!
Well, gee, okay!
I think he wants to be my friend.
Too bad recess has to end.

Ogden Nash
# The Adventures of Isabel

Isabel met an enormous bear,
Isabel, Isabel, didn't care;
The bear was hungry, the bear was ravenous,
The bear's big mouth was cruel and cavernous.
The bear said, "Isabel, glad to meet you,
How do, Isabel, now I'll eat you!"
Isabel, Isabel, didn't worry,
Isabel didn't scream or scurry.
She washed her hands and she straightened her hair up,
Then Isabel quietly ate the bear up.

Once in a night as black as pitch
Isabel met a wicked old witch.
The witch's face was cross and wrinkled,
The witch's gums with teeth were sprinkled.
"Ho ho, Isabel!" the old witch crowed,
"I'll turn you into an ugly toad!"
Isabel, Isabel, didn't worry,
Isabel didn't scream or scurry.
She showed no rage and showed no rancor,
But she turned the witch into milk and drank her.

Isabel met a hideous giant,
Isabel continued self-reliant.
The giant was hairy, the giant was horrid,
He had one eye in the middle of his forehead.
"Good morning, Isabel," the giant said,
"I'll grind your bones to make my bread."
Isabel, Isabel, didn't worry,
Isabel didn't scream or scurry.
She nibbled the zwieback that she always fed off,
And when it was gone, she cut the giant's head off.

Isabel met a troublesome doctor,
He punched and he poked till he really shocked her.
The doctor's talk was of coughs and chills
And the doctor's satchel bulged with pills.
The doctor said unto Isabel,
"Swallow this, it will make you well."
Isabel, Isabel, didn't worry,
Isabel didn't scream or scurry.
She took those pills from the pill concocter,
And Isabel calmly cured the doctor.

Isabel once was asleep in bed
When a horrible dream crawled into her head.
It was worse than a dinosaur, worse than a shark,
Worse than an octopus oozing in the dark.
"Boo!" said the dream, with a dreadful grin,
"I'm going to scare you out of your skin!"
Isabel, Isabel, didn't worry,
Isabel didn't scream or scurry.
Isabel had a cleverer scheme;
She just woke up and fooled that dream.

Whenever you meet a bugaboo
Remember what Isabel used to do.
Don't scream when the bugaboo says "Boo!"
Just look it in the eye and say, "Boo to you!"
That's how to banish a bugaboo;
Isabel did it and you can too!
"Boooooo to you!"

# Index of Authors

# Index of Titles

# Copyright Acknowledgments

Sometimes I get scared about a wolf coming into my room. So I think about it wearing silly underwear and a funny hat.

I'm afraid of barking dogs with big teeth. Now I go the other way, but if I can't, I